You Got a Phone!

(Now Read This Book)

Elizabeth K. Englander, Ph.D.,
and Katharine Covino, Ed.D.

Illustrated by Steve Mark

free spirit
PUBLISHING®

Library of Congress Cataloging-in-Publication Data
Names: Englander, Elizabeth Kandel, author. | Covino, Katharine, author. | Mark, Steve, illustrator.
Title: You got a phone! : (now read this book) / Elizabeth K. Englander, Ph.D. and Katharine Covino, Ed.D. ; illustrated by Steve Mark.
Description: Minneapolis, MN : Free Spirit Publishing, Inc., [2022] | Series: Laugh & learn | Includes index. | Audience: Ages 8–13
Identifiers: LCCN 2021039509 (print) | LCCN 2021039510 (ebook) | ISBN 9781631986406 (paperback) | ISBN 9781631986413 (pdf) | ISBN 9781631986420 (epub)
Subjects: LCSH: Smartphones and children—Juvenile literature. | Smartphones—Psychological aspects—Juvenile literature. | Smartphones—Social aspects—Juvenile literature. | Children—Effect of technological innovations on—Juvenile literature.
Classification: LCC HQ784.S54 E54 2022 (print) | LCC HQ784.S54 (ebook) | DDC 004.167083—dc23
LC record available at https://lccn.loc.gov/2021039509
LC ebook record available at https://lccn.loc.gov/2021039510

Reading Level Grade 5; Interest Level Ages 8–13;
Fountas & Pinnell Guided Reading Level T

Edited by Eric Braun and Christine Zuchora-Walske
Cover and interior design by Emily Dyer
Illustrated by Steve Mark

10 9 8 7 6 5 4 3 2 1
Printed in China
R18860222

Free Spirit Publishing Inc.
6325 Sandburg Road, Suite 100
Minneapolis, MN 55427-3674
(612) 338-2068
help4kids@freespirit.com
freespirit.com

Dedication

We dedicate this book to our six children, who helped teach us the pitfalls and joys of kids owning phones:

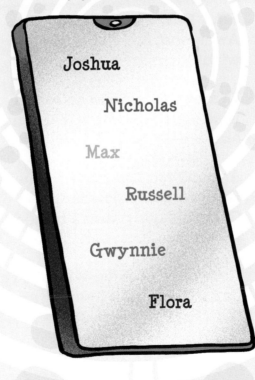

Joshua

Nicholas

Max

Russell

Gwynnie

Flora

Contents

Chapter 1
Your New Phone Is Totally Awesome: But It Comes with Buts

Sometimes it's great to be last. The last person to be kidnapped by aliens! The last person to be eaten by zombies!

But other times it stinks to be last—literally. Have you ever been last in line at camp to use the bathroom? Remember that smell? Not so delightful.

And maybe you felt like you were the last person on Earth to get your own phone. Maybe you thought all that waiting really stunk. Well, you're not waiting anymore. That's because . . .

You finally got a phone!

Now you can text your friends! You can chat in apps, record music videos, and play games! You can grow your list of followers! You can watch videos about three-toed sloths and impress your friends with your amazing new knowledge!

3

You can take RI-DIC-U-LOUS pictures and send them. A picture of your dog wearing a tutu and barrettes. A picture of your sister sleeping in the car with drool running down her chin. A picture of you and your friends (and your cat) using all kinds of Insta-filters. You can listen to music, follow your favorite athletes, research nuclear submarines, learn how to fix your bike, and lots more. The world is literally at your fingertips. That's because . . .

You! Got! A! Phone!

Big BUTs

Even if you didn't wait long or you didn't feel like you were last, it's still pretty exciting. However, when it comes to phones, that excitement comes with a few buts—*big buts*.

Your new phone is super fun, BUT . . .

Some kids find that their phone can suck all their time and attention, kind of like a super-sucky digital black hole. Their phones are so intensely interesting that these kids have a hard time keeping up with other things like chores, homework, playing with pets, and hanging out with friends and family.

Your phone is really convenient, BUT . . .

Sometimes it can cause problems. Friends can misunderstand each other or get mad about something that probably wouldn't be a big deal in person. Sometimes it seems like the wrong emoji can start the next world war.

Your phone is an incredibly creative tool, BUT . . .

It can be easy to make mistakes that end up hurting someone else—or yourself. Sometimes you share a photo you shouldn't have, or you say something you later regret.

Your phone is amazingly useful, BUT . . .

You pay for that usefulness by giving up some of your privacy. This can be a big deal, so it's smart to learn something about it.

You Can't Ride Your Phone, BUT....

It turns out that getting a phone is like getting a bike: It's something you have to learn to use.

What's that you say? You're shocked? You've been using phones, tablets, computers, and other devices forever. What's there to learn about?

Well, learning helps you avoid problems and stay out of trouble. Learning can also help you get the most out of your phone, so you can truly enjoy its awesome powers. That's what this book is all about. And lucky for you, learning does not have to be boring. If you've ever watched a grown-up learn to snowboard, you know it can be *hilarious*.

FASCINATING FACT

Did you know your phone is a more powerful computer than the Apollo computer that first put people on the moon way back in 1969? In fact, it has about 100,000 times the processing power—all in the palm of your hand.

Okay, so chances are you won't be helping people land on the moon. But you probably will be doing some pretty critical communication. Maybe something like Jane and Jamal here.

The chapters of this book are all designed to help you learn to be in control of your phone, not the other way around.

Also, there's some weird stuff about flying pie . . . you'll see.

Rules and Phone Phreedom

Your parent ✱, or whoever gave you your phone, might have talked to you about the rules for using it. Maybe you signed a contract or agreement promising to follow those rules. Rules can be tough, like overcooked chicken. But having the DOs and DON'Ts laid out can be really helpful. That way you know what's okay and what's not. You know when you can use your phone, and for how long. You stay out of trouble and keep your freedom—your Phone Phreedom, that is.

✱ When you see *parent* or *parents* in this book, think of the person or people who take care of you. That might be a mom, a dad, a foster parent or stepparent, a grandparent, another family adult, or someone else. Think of the person who is the most responsible for you and who probably gave you that fancy phone.

If your parent hasn't talked to you about this yet, the next page has six guidelines you can follow on your own. Consider them the basic rules for phone behavior. Following these can (a) help keep you safe online with a healthy life balance; (b) keep your parents cool, calm, and collected; and (c) ensure that you get to keep using your awesome new phone.

6 BASIC PHONE RULES

1 Whatever conditions your parents put on using the phone, accept them. Don't argue, even if the rules seem unfair or too strict. After you've shown your parents how responsible you can be, you can consider asking to change things.

2 Homework first, chores second, and screens third . . . maybe. If your parent says it's okay. Doing your homework and chores shows your parent that you're responsible enough to have a phone.

3 If your parent calls or texts, answer them. That's just basic respect. (If you can't answer right away, like because you're in a movie theater or class, get back to them as soon as you can.)

4 Remember that your smartphone is connected to the internet, which means you need to be careful. Don't go to websites you know you shouldn't go to. Don't click on a link that says you get a prize for being the 100th visitor to the site. Strangers who say they want to make you a model or a star are not telling the truth. There is no prince desperate to share his money with you. Don't worry, though. A little common sense is all you need. Reading this book will help.

. . . .

5 Be kind. Remember that those are humans on the other end of your communications, and they have feelings.

. . . .

6 Finally, remember that the person who pays for the phone is the person who actually owns it. That's . . . let's see . . . probably not you. Which means your parent might read your texts or check your history sometimes. That's their right, and they're not doing it to be nosy. (Well, maybe a little.) They're doing it to help keep you healthy and safe. In the meantime, **you get to use that awesome phone!** And that's pretty great.

Bonus
Download

→ Because it's so easy and quick to send messages to your friends, sometimes people get a little careless, and that can cause hurt feelings. So, be careful what you send and what you post! Take your time and choose your words carefully. Always think about how others might feel when they read or see what you post.

→ It's easy to lose track of the time you spend with your phone—so try to notice! Look up from your device every few minutes and remember to appreciate the world around you.

→ Perhaps one of the reasons that elephants have such gigantic rear ends is that they eat so much. The average elephant eats between 300 and 600 pounds of food each day! In fact, they spend about 16 hours eating every day. Imagine if all your waking hours were devoted to eating. Now that would be quite a life!

Chapter 2

Drama-rama: How to Avoid Muddled Misunderstandings and Messy Magnifications

You probably know how it feels to have an argument or fight with a friend. It feels . . . *blech*. Luckily, most of the time you can talk things through and make up. Life goes on. But sometimes there's real *drama*. That can mean anger, regret, hurt feelings, or sadness. Sometimes the drama gets so bad, you need a bigger word just to contain it all. Let's call it *drama-rama*.

What does this have to do with phones? Phones make communication between people easy. You can text, post, and play games with your friends anytime, which is *awesome*. Tap a few buttons and, *shoom*, there goes your message. But because it's so easy to communicate, it's also easy to MIS-communicate.

There are two main ways that miscommunicating on phones can cause drama, or even drama-rama, with friends, family, and others. They are Muddled Misunderstandings and Messy Magnifications.

Read on to learn more about these sticky situations and how to avoid drama-rama (and llamas in the Bahamas).

Muddled Misunderstandings

Misunderstanding each other when you text is common. This might seem hard to believe. After all, people text all the time. (Seriously: All. The. Time.) How can it cause big problems?

Good question—glad you asked!

The reason texting is so easy and fast is because it's a shortcut. Ever try to make cupcakes using just eggs and flour? If you don't use all the other ingredients (butter, vanilla, sugar), you'll still get something that is sort of like cupcakes, but they won't taste the same. Your cupcakes will be *yuck*-cakes. The things that were missing were actually important. Texting is sort of like that, but for conversations. You get fewer words and maybe some acronyms and emojis, but you don't get the full message. You're missing some key ingredients.

One problem is that you can't *see* the other person. So you don't get all those other ingredients—oops, clues— such as their facial expression and body language. If your friend calls you a jerk, that might hurt your feelings. But if she says it with a big, friendly smile that lets you know she's only teasing, that's very different. You know she doesn't mean it. But if she says it in a text message, where you can't see her big smile, you might not get that she's joking.

Or imagine you text your friend "Good game today," and he texts back "Thanks a lot." That could mean just what it says: thanks. Or maybe your friend is feeling bad about how he did in the soccer game today, and he thinks you're making fun of him. His *thanks a lot* might actually be sarcastic. What he really means is that you hurt his feelings. If you are talking in person, you can see that he feels bad. He might be looking at the ground, or he might give you a hurt expression. If he does, you'll notice right away and you can fix it by saying something like, "No, I mean it! That was a great corner kick in the second half."

Another missing ingredient when texting is tone of voice. The sound of how a person talks can change the meaning of what they say, even if they use the exact same words. Don't believe it? Check out this simple sentence. When the tone and emphasis change, the whole meaning changes.

What you said & how you said it	How your tone and emphasis changed what you meant
I didn't toot during your piano recital.	Somebody sure tooted, but it wasn't me.
I didn't *toot* during your piano recital.	Well, I didn't toot. Let's first be clear on that point. But I may have done something else.
I didn't toot *during* your piano recital.	Yes, I tooted. But it wasn't during your recital. It was before. Nobody was playing music yet. (Well, I suppose I was playing music of a sort.)
I didn't toot during your *piano recital.*	I tooted, but it didn't happen during your piano recital. It happened another time.

If you had this gaseous conversation in person, your friend would be able to hear which word you spoke louder and longer than the others. They would also hear your tone of voice. If you sounded angry, that might tell them that you're mad they mentioned the tooting incident. If you sounded sorry, they might forgive you. If you laughed, they might laugh along. (Or they might be mad that you're not taking this seriously!)

But, just like you can't see body language and facial expressions when you're texting, you also can't hear tone of voice. Without that extra information, people can easily misunderstand each other. You might *think* you know what someone means, but you could be wrong.

Messy Magnifications

It's not just Muddled Misunderstandings that can lead you astray. Phones can also magnify things—and sometimes that leads to problems.

Imagine taking a selfie. You know that you have to hold the phone just the right way. If you're too far away, no one will notice your amazing haircut. But being too close might be even worse. If the camera isn't held right, you might magnify the wrong thing! Unless you're someone who prizes close-up photos of the bottom half of your left nostril.

Just as your phone's camera can magnify your face into a warped piece of modern art, texting and messaging can magnify your thoughts, ideas, and feelings. Maybe you're a little worried about your next math test. But spend an hour texting with friends about how hard it's going to be, and suddenly that "little worried" has turned into such deep worry that you can't sleep.

Why does this happen? Why do messages and posts sometimes result in intensified and magnified feelings?

It has to do with the way you're communicating. When you talk to someone in person or in a phone call, you say your words out loud. The other person hears them, and then those words are gone. *Whoosh!* Swept away into the ether. People might remember the words, but they don't have to look at them anymore.

But when you're texting or messaging on your phone, words don't disappear. They stay right where they are. And you might look at them over and over.

Imagine you're at the park with a friend and you get in a fight. You're face to face. And let's say you both say some hurtful things. You're not proud of it, but it happened. You both heard each other's hurtful words— but just once. No, it wasn't good. Yes, you'll both have to apologize and try to make things better between you. But at least it only happened once.

Now, imagine that you're in the fight with the same friend, but this time you're texting, not talking. You're both sitting at home staring at your screens. The hurtful words come in, you read them, and then . . . they're still there, on-screen. You read them again. You get mad again. Maybe you try to cool off by putting down your phone. But then you pick it up and read the argument again, because it's just bugging you so much.

Reading the messages over and over can actually make your feelings about what's there BIGGER.

This can happen with good things too. If you and your friend are texting about your exciting plans for a sleepover, that good thing can become stupendous.

Muddled Misunderstandings and Messy Magnifications `when having a text conversation` mean that sometimes you can hurt someone's feelings, have your own feelings hurt, or even get into a fight with someone—all by accident.

Jane: Lucy is always mad at me. I can tell from her texts.

Jamal: What did she say?

Jane: "I know."

Jamal: You know what?

Jane: No, she said, "I know."

Jamal: Oh. Well that doesn't sound like she's mad. She just is letting you know she knows.

Jane: That's not how it sounded to me.

Jamal: Wait—what did it "sound" like?

Jane: You know.

Jamal: It sounded like "you know"?

Jane: No, I mean *you know*. You know?

Jamal: No.

How to Avoid Drama-rama

If you notice that a text or message conversation is getting heated, you can cool it down before things get out of hand—and before your misunderstanding becomes drama. Or the dreaded drama-rama.

First, remember that misunderstandings can go both ways. Maybe you aren't sure if your friend Allison really likes or really *doesn't like* your idea of inviting both boys and girls to your birthday party. When she texted, it wasn't clear to you. But at the same time, Allison might be wondering why you made that snarky comment about her favorite Taylor Swift song. Did you mean to be funny? Did you really not like it? Try to be as clear as you can in your communication, and don't be surprised if someone is confused by something you text. It happens to everyone.

Second, try seeing things from the other person's point of view. If a friend texts something that's confusing or hurtful, put yourself in his position. Is it possible that your friend made a mistake? Could that mean text actually be read a different way—a way that is NOT so mean? If you're not sure, there's one way to find out: Ask.

"Why did you LOL at my picture?"

"Are you upset?"

Did they really mean to make fun of my hedgehog toy?

The third thing you can do when message exchanges start to get heated is slow down. Take your time and think about your responses. If someone's text is making you really mad or upset, don't answer right away. Put the phone down and take a break for at least a few minutes. Think about how important your friendship is, and think of exactly how you want to reply. Be calm when you do.

Basic misunderstandings are bad enough, but a bigger problem is when confusion leads to a fight—or an all-out text brawl. Sometimes you find yourself fighting or arguing with a close friend over messages you've exchanged, and you're not even sure what you're fighting about, how it started, or why everyone is so stinkin' mad.

When texting turns into a text brawl, it's time to put the brakes on the conversation. No more texting. What can you do instead?

If only there were a way to actually *talk* to your friends. If only . . .

Ah, good thinking! There *is* a way. You can make a phone call. Hey, it is called a *phone*, right? Tell your friend you're confused by what's happening, and ask if they can talk. Then, give them a call and explain your feelings. Better yet, use video calling so you can see each other. That way all those facial expressions come through. If you're feeling bad about something your friend said, they will be able to see it for themselves. And you can see how they are feeling too.

Or wait! You can do even better.

You could talk in real life.

Yes, it's true. You can put your phone down and seek out the other person IRL. That is the best way to make sure you both understand each other.

Bonus
Download

→ When you can't see or hear someone, you might think they're saying one thing when really they mean something else. Tone of voice is a key tool for interpreting and understanding what someone is saying. But tone of voice is missing when you message or text online.

→ Feelings can get really big and really messy when you're using your phone. Like, you can get really mad, even though someone else isn't trying to make you mad.

→ You know how you can sometimes feel stressed or worried when you get a text or a message in ALL CAPS? ALL CAPS means shouting today, but did you know that the first computers had *no lowercase letters at all?* It's like they only knew how to shout, and not to talk. Imagine how relieved these computers must have been when lowercase letters were finally invented. After a lifetime of SHOUTING, they could just speak in a more normal tone of voice.

Chapter 3

About That Last Rib-B-Que: Understanding Bullying, Cyberbullying, and Phone-y Meanness

How are phones like food fights?

Well, some people think they're both a lot of fun. You probably agree that your smartphone is fun. As for food fights . . . imagine you're in the middle of a big one. A truly epic display of strategy and cunning, and a breathtaking use of honey mustard.

Fun?

That depends how much you like honey mustard in your ear.

A more important way that phones are like food fights is that they both can make grown-ups a little . . . nervous. You can see why food fights might make adults a little antsy in their pantsy. Food fights are messy. If things get out of control, people can get hurt. (Imagine being bonked by a banana!)

Smartphones are the same way. They can also be very messy. And they can result in people getting hurt.

It's Easy Being Mean

What is it about phones that sometimes makes them as messy as a flying blueberry pie?

You've read about how phones make it easy to communicate, and how because of that, sometimes we MIS-communicate. That's messy enough. But on top of that, phones can also make it easy to be mean.

That's *really* messy.

Sometimes it's an accident. We send messages or post comments without totally thinking it through. You might just dash off a message, like about how your friend's sweater looks just like one your grandma has. You don't think it will be hurtful. It's just a joke, but your friend takes it to heart. When that happens, you can apologize to your friend. Get on the phone or talk in person to make sure your friend can see that you're sincere.

Sometimes, though, hurting someone is not a mistake at all. Sometimes people use their phones to intentionally be mean to others.

Maybe you're thinking this would never happen to you.

I just use it to text and game!

I only talk to my friends!

My phone is so fun!

You might be right. A lot of kids say they never experience meanness on their phone. But plenty of kids do. What if it *does* happen to you?

There's a lot you can do to protect yourself from cruel comments, mean messages, and nasty notes on your phone. (No, you don't have to wear protective armor.) A lot depends on the type of malicious missives coming in, and who is involved. Sometimes it's being mean. Sometimes it's cyberbullying.

Being Mean Vs. Cyberbullying

Bullying is when someone is mean to someone else, on purpose, with the intention of hurting them, over and over again. When bullying happens on your phone or digital device, it is called cyberbullying.

Cyberbullying could be someone sending you mean messages on your phone, over and over. Or someone who takes pictures of you every day and posts them, making fun of you. If someone repeatedly puts mean or pestering comments on your social media, that's cyberbullying too.

It might seem like cyberbullying wouldn't be as bad as bullying face-to-face. You don't have to see the other person. But cyberbullying can be scary and hurtful. One reason is that you have your phone with you most of the time. Cyberbullying can reach you everywhere you go. So you might see something mean anywhere: at school, at hockey practice, even at home. Even in your safest place, like your bedroom, those messages can come in—ping!— and find you.

PING

Not only that, cyberbullying sometimes feels worse than other kinds of bullying because there's often a big audience. If someone is posting cruel comments in a group chat or on social media, lots of people might see it. It can feel like everyone is in on a big joke at your expense. You can feel really alone.

You need to know about cyberbullying in case someone does it to you. You also need to understand it to make sure that you don't do it to someone else.

To help you understand whether something is cyberbullying, here's a test.

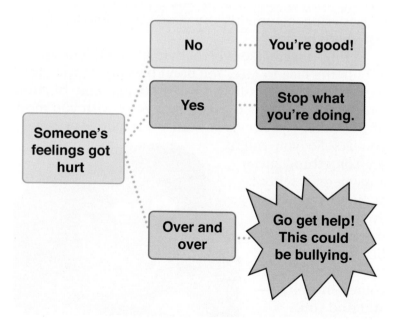

FASCINATING FACT

If you lined up four kids in a row, at least one of them has probably been cyberbullied.

So What Can You Do About It?

Is someone being mean on the phone?

If someone is being mean to you, but a part of you suspects that it might be a misunderstanding, talking is the solution! Ask the person to talk to you in person to see what they really mean. Did they *mean* to be mean?

If someone is being mean on purpose, that's not something you want to keep a secret. The thing about bullying and meanness is it doesn't always stop immediately. But you can always work—immediately!—to make it less painful. What might make you feel better? Talking about it with your friends, for one. Ask your friends to make a pact with you: You all promise to talk to each other if anyone is being mean or is bullying on your phones. Just being there for each other and talking about it can help kids feel better. You can also stick up for each other if the hurtful stuff is happening on social media, group chats, or other public forums.

You can also talk to all the other people who love you and care about you. That might be your brothers and sisters, your parents, your doctor, or your grandma! These people are there for you, and talking to them will make the meanness sting less.

Parents and other adults can be an especially important resource. Be sure to tell them if the meanness is really making you feel sad or worried. An adult can also help you change settings on your phone to help with the problem. You can block certain people from texting you or from reading or posting on your social media. You can make your accounts private.

Can adults handle *all* your phone problems? Yes and no. Sometimes, it is not cool to tell an adult. If someone gets to the lunch line ahead of you and gets the last rib-b-que, you should NOT tell an adult. That's just fair play. If you want that rib-b-que, you can do what everyone else does and hurry like heck to the lunch line. If you're too late, you can just suck it up and have a cold sandwich.

If, however, someone is being mean to you intentionally and repeatedly, then it's important to tell an adult.

And it isn't just other people that can help you feel better. You can take the reindeer by the horns and make yourself feel better too. Do things that are physical and distracting. Take a break from your phone and go outside. Read a book with your dad. Make dinner with your mom. Hang out with other people who like you. Eat lunch with your friends. Play board games. Swing on the tire swing. Take another run at the Gaga Ball championship. Get yourself some snuggles and cuddles with your parents or grandparents. Or hug your pet (as long as it's not a pet cactus).

Bonus
Download

→ Sometimes kids get mean messages from others. At times, it's really by mistake, but other times, it can be on purpose. When it happens over and over again, that's *cyberbullying*.

→ People being mean and fighting online is one of those problems you definitely don't want to hide or keep to yourself. Talk to your friends, your family, or other people you like and trust. Even just talking can help a lot.

→ One of the biggest and most famous food fights happens every year in Spain. The *La Tomatina* festival is an epic battle that begins with a ceremonial "hoisting of the ham." With the ham hanging proudly atop a flagpole, thousands of food fighters fling almost 200,000 tomatoes at each other for over an hour. How *totally awesome* is that?

Chapter 4

New and Creative Ways to Freak Out Grown-ups: Posting and Sharing Pictures Online

Imagine that there was a "Throw Me Up" app. No, it wouldn't be about puking—that would be both strange and gross. No, the Throw Me Up app would dare people to throw their cell phones as high as they could up in the air, and then the app would measure how high the phones went.

Ha-ha! Super fun and challenging, you say. Where can a person download this delightful app? What could possibly go wrong with such a rollicking and free-spirited pastime? What could possibly be the downside?

Wait for it.

It's coming.

It's nearly there.

Aha! You've got it.

What goes up, must come

DOWN

But even though you know this imaginary app would be a disaster waiting to happen, it could still be *amazingly* popular. Why? Sometimes people do things that seem fun in the short term, and they don't think about the downside—even when it's really obvious. Throwing up a basketball is fun. Throwing up a phone is BONKERS.

At first, when your friend challenges you to a phone throwing contest, it might sound okay. The first throw goes well. You're in the lead. But, inevitably, after a few throws, your phone splats like an egg, and the fun is immediately over.

Hey, Be Careful with That Phone!

Clearly you would never do this. You're no phone-flinging fool. So what does this imaginary, truly foolish Throw Me Up app have to do with you and *your* phone?

The answer has to do with posting pictures online. At first, it can be exciting and thrilling! Your friend posts a picture of his little sister asleep in her spaghetti. Then, you post a picture of your brother picking his nose. Each outrageous picture is outclassed by another picture that's EVEN OUTRAGEOUS-ER. Lots of people are liking and sharing your photos and everyone seems to be having fun.

As you might guess, things can very quickly spiral out of control. In the process of finding wilder and wilder photos to post and share, you could cross a line. There are at least three ways that things can go wrong in the world of photo snapping and posting.

You could hurt someone's feelings. Posting a picture of your sister asleep in her spaghetti might be funny—to you. But sharing things that are supposed to be private could really hurt someone's feelings. Think about how your sister—or whoever is in your photo—would feel if you shared that silly photo.

You could make yourself look bad. Another problem is that something that you think is innocent and funny might be gross or even upsetting to someone else. As hard as it is to believe, not everyone has a deep appreciation for shots of toddlers drooling while asleep in their dinner. Think about the reaction the picture might get. What might folks think about you—the person who shared it? Depending on the photo, they might think that you acted selfishly. They might think you're mean. You could even get in trouble.

It could stay there forever. A big problem with putting pictures—or anything else—online is that sometimes those things *stay* online. Forever. Pictures can be copied and kept by anybody who sees them. So, if you post a picture of a drooling toddler, you lose control of that photo. You might forget about it pretty quickly, but lots of people could see it in the future, even if you end up deleting your post. Maybe just when you're hoping to get that babysitting job!

Say Cheese—Uh, Make That PLEASE

There are a few good ways to make sure you don't cross a line when taking and posting photos. They all involve asking questions.

Ask the person in the photo if it's okay. Actually, ask them *before* they are in the photo—ask them if it's okay to take a picture of them. After you take it, maybe you want to post it. Maybe you got a terrific shot of your buddy doing a cannonball at the pool. But even if it's a terrific shot, it's possible your friend does not want that picture out in the world. Make sure you ask someone *before* you post or share that photo.

It doesn't matter if you're posting a picture on social media, putting it on your blog or website, or just texting it to someone else, anytime you send a photo in any way to any location, you are "sharing" it, and you need to ask permission first. This is true even if you didn't take the photo yourself. If someone else sent it to you and you want to post it or send it on to others, ask first.

That also goes for photos that aren't of the person but are of something that belongs to them or is associated with them. This includes things like their bedroom or home, their belongings, even their family members. You might think that picture of a pet pig in a hat is super cute, but maybe the owner doesn't want others to see that. You don't know! That's why you have to ask.

Ask yourself why you want to share the photo. If your friend is doing a gnarly wheelie on their bike, and you want to share their AWESOMENESS with others, that's a great reason to share. It shows that you think your friend is doing something cool. Show your friend the picture you took; they will probably say yes.

On the other hand, if you think your friend's haircut looks like he dried it with a leaf blower, your motives aren't quite so kind. All the more reason to check with your friend before taking a photo of that tumbleweed on his head—and *definitely* ask before sharing it. Some people are confident enough that they are willing to laugh at themselves. If that's your friend, maybe he'll say yes. If so, try to be kind even if you make a gentle joke.

Asking yourself why you want to post that photo can usually give you a good clue to whether it's a good idea. If your reasons are not so kind, there's a good chance you should not post that photo. If your reasons *are* kind, or at least fair, you're probably in the clear. But you should still check with the other person.

AH
CHOO

Ask yourself what the consequences could be. Is this photo funny or is it disgusting? Even if it's both, is it too gross for public consumption? Would you feel differently if *you* were in the picture? What if this stays on the internet FOR-EV-ER? What if people find out you posted it? Are you cool with that? Give all of these questions some thought.

Ask your granny. Okay, you don't have to actually call your grandma every time you want to take a photo. Instead, you simply *imagine* your grandma is going to see the photo. What would she think?

Imagine you take that perfect photo. That real prize-winning shot just after your baby brother sneezed midway through his jar of peas, just at the moment your father, oh your poor father, was coming in with the helicopter spoon to deliver another load. Dad is covered in a rare mixture of baby snot and baby peas. Your big brother is laughing. Your father is crying. And you, lucky you, you've got your phone out at just the right moment to capture this brilliant moment. You've got it—the best, funniest, grossest pic of all time!

Now, before you pop that beauty up on social or shoot it off to your youth group chat, take a pause. Imagine your granny is going to see this photo. What would that kind, gentle, loving woman think?

This is a nice, simple, one-step way of thinking of all those consequences you just read about. It's a shortcut. Think of it as the Granny Test. If it's okay with the people in the photo, and with Granny, it's okay for *you*.

By the way, if you don't have a grandmother, you can imagine someone else's grandmother. Or an imaginary little old lady who has your best interests at heart. It also can be useful to ask a friend. No, not *that* friend—the one who's always doing dumb stuff and getting in trouble. Some other friend. Ask the friend who your mom thinks is nice.

Posting Photos of Your Favorite Subject: You

Of course, often, the most fun photos to post are photos of yourself! After all, who doesn't like seeing pictures of themselves online? Like that year when you and your friends did that whole group superhero costume for Halloween. Now, that was spectacular!

But just like with pictures of other people, it's important to be thoughtful and smart about what photos you post of yourself. Ask yourself a few questions: Is there a chance you'll regret posting this photo? Would you be okay with *anyone in the world* seeing it? Or with it staying on the internet forever? Whether capturing yourself or the whole group of superheroes, it's important to ask yourself questions before sharing.

It's also important to never share photos or personal information online with someone you don't know.

THE INTERNET'S NOT PRIVATE. LIKE EVER.

REALLY NEVER PRIVATE.

Photos aren't the only thing that aren't private on the internet. Any information you put online can be seen, copied, and forwarded. You never know when someone is going to screenshot your info, your comment, your photo, or something else you post. Not only that, apps and websites track your clicks and other data. Companies use this information to learn more about you so they can send you ads for things they think you'll buy. Sometimes, being on a phone can *feel* private because you're alone when you look at it. You're often in a private place like your bedroom. But always remember: Once you post it, it's out of your control. You never know who's going to see it. So choose wisely.

Bonus
Download

→ Being able to take pictures is one of the best things about having a phone, but it also sometimes causes problems, like hurting people's feelings or making you look silly.

→ If someone else is in the picture, ask them if it's okay to share it. And ask yourself *why* you want to share it. Friendly motives are the only way to go!

→ So, you're interested in taking and sharing photos? Fantastic! For inspiration, check out some of these award-winning pictures, all taken by kids just like you! natgeokids.com/uk/kids -club/cool-kids/general-kids-club/nat-geo-kids -photo-comp-2019

Chapter 5

Oh No, It's FOMO: When Your Phone Causes Stress or Anxiety

Once upon a time there was a young boy who really, really wanted to go on the Tilt-A-Whirl. He'd seen his older brother go on it for years, and his brother always laughed and howled with delight. Then, that fabulous July day arrived when the boy was finally tall enough to go on the ride. He bought his ticket. He stood in line. He got buckled in. The ride started. His stomach filled with butterflies. It was fun. He could just feel his coolness factor going, up . . . up . . . up. And then . . .

Oh, no . . .

Those butterflies got dizzy in his stomach, and something else started coming up-up-up.

Yup. Just like that, something awesome changed into something . . . less awesome.

Smartphones can be kind of like that. Mostly they're fun. Occasionally, though, phones can make you feel bad. Sometimes you can even feel it in your stomach.

All About Anxiety

Anxiety means worry. Everyone feels worried sometimes. Maybe you feel it when the teacher says he's going to return the history test at the end of class. All you can think about is that test. Feeling worry like this is totally common. It would be hard to grow up without feeling a little worried now and then. In fact, a little worry can be good—it can help you prepare for important things. Think about that nervous feeling you get when you have a big basketball game or recital coming up. If it's important to you, you're going to worry about it, and that worry might lead you to practice harder. Then you end up doing better. Thanks, worry!

But anxiety is more than regular worry. Anxiety is like feeling worried *plus*. When you feel like you can't focus on your schoolwork because you're so worried, or you can't fall asleep or relax, or you question your own worth, and that feeling won't go away—that's anxiety. Experts describe anxiety as a feeling of worry about something that could happen, something you imagine might happen, or something that happened in the past. And phones are really good at creating anxiety.

Maybe you send someone an important message and you keep checking your phone for a reply, over and over. You check—no reply. A bit later you check—no reply. And so on. And you can't understand why your friend didn't reply. Is he mad at you? Is he ignoring you? WHAT IS GOING ON?

If you're old enough to be on social media, you might find yourself scrolling through pictures of people doing awesome things, like taking trips to amazing places or showing off their cool new clothes. Or maybe you see photo after photo of people who look beautiful or strong or happy or just . . . perfect. You keep comparing your own life to theirs, and when you do, your life seems boring and, well, regular. You want to stop looking, but for some reason you just keep scrolling. And the more you scroll, the worse you feel.

Or maybe your friends post photos from their slumber party, and you feel bad that they didn't invite you. You keep asking yourself questions like, *Did they forget me, or leave me out on purpose? Why would they leave me out? What's wrong with me?*

That's a special kind of anxiety that's known as FOMO: Fear of Missing Out. Feeling left out is not weird or unusual. No matter how many friends, "likes," or followers you have, you will still get left out sometimes. It's a guarantee.

Jane: What's up?

Jamal: I checked out social media and I saw that Kyle and Matt were sledding together. When I saw them I felt bad.

Jane: They didn't invite me either. Maybe you and I could go sledding.

Jamal: Good idea. I guess I don't feel as bad. Speaking of feeling bad, did I ever tell you about when I went on that Tilt-A-Whirl? It all started when I had a super huge breakfast.

Jane: Yes, Jamal. You have definitely told me.

The Illusions Created by Phone World

Anxiety and FOMO might be normal. That doesn't mean they're fun. They don't feel good. FOMO can lead to FOGS (Feelings Of Gloomy Sadness). Also to FASD (Frustration And Self-Doubt). Not to mention FRUCATA (Feeling Really Uncomfortable, Cruddy, And Totally Awful).

Anxiety and FOMO have always been around, but cell phones have made them more common. You see, back in olden times, people didn't carry phones. Each home had a phone attached to the wall. And all you could do was talk on it! The most fun you could have with this thing was when you got to untangle the super long curly cord! (If you don't know what a phone cord is, do an internet search for pictures—it'll blow your mind.) If you wanted to talk to your friend Samantha about your new iguana, you had to call her phone and hope someone at Samantha's home heard it ring and picked it up. If they didn't, maybe you could leave a message—if they had an answering machine. (Again: do a search!) If they didn't, you just had to keep calling back until someone picked up.

Nowadays, lots of people are carrying their phones in their pocket all the time. That creates an illusion that others are always ready to talk or text, any old time. But that's *not true.* Sometimes when you send a text, the other person might not respond right away because they're in the shower. Or eating dinner with their family. Or reading a book, taking a walk, or riding a bike. You might feel like you're being ignored. You might be waiting for that notification to go *ping,* telling you that you got a reply. But the truth is, the other person might just be living their life. If they're not responding to your message, it doesn't necessarily mean that they're ignoring you on purpose.

Another illusion that phones can create is that of perfection. People are usually very careful to only post words and photos that make themselves look beautiful, cool, tough, smart, or in some way great. You rarely see anybody post a photo with the caption, "Look at this huge zit!" You don't often see someone post about their normal failures or shortcomings, like, "I got a terrible grade on my book report."

Instead, most posts and photos are carefully designed to make the person appear their best. They talk about great things they did or that happened to them: "Here's the amazing beach where we are on vacation!" "Here's my science project I worked really hard on and I got an award for!" If someone posts a selfie, they most likely planned their look and snapped many photos before picking the best one. They may have carefully done their makeup and used fancy filters to make themselves look even better. When you come across someone's adorable selfie, you don't think about all the work that went into it. All you see is the result. It looks easy. It looks like they are perfect.

As a result, when you scroll through your phone, you end up seeing lots and lots of posts and photos that make everyone look amazing and their lives look exciting and fun. You probably even know that people do this—put their best self online—but you still can't help comparing yourself to them. All of which can end up making you feel bad about yourself.

Fighting FOMO and Abolishing Anxiety

So you know it's not true that everyone's life is perfect except for yours. You know the illusion of everyone having fun online without you is not real . . . but maybe it still *feels* real. If you're feeling worried that you weren't invited somewhere or that someone is ignoring you, or if you're feeling like your ordinary life just doesn't compare to the lives of others you see online, there are things you can do to help yourself feel better.

Exercising, for example. If you've been sitting around with your phone all day feeling anxious or left out, use exercise to help get rid of those feelings. It will help activate *endorphins* in your brain that will make you feel better. Endorphins are awesome chemicals that live in your brain and are released by exercise. They're like the best sugar rush ever!

Distract yourself. Play your flute, take a shower, bake cookies, paint pottery, sew a superhero costume, or do a crossword or jigsaw puzzle. Things like this don't only distract you from your yucky feelings. They also build something positive. Playing an instrument helps you improve at that instrument. Baking or doing art is creative. Puzzles improve your brain power. Even taking a shower is positive—especially if you're stinky.

Do something with others. In person. Get together with a friend. Invite your sister to bake those cookies with you. Ask your mom or dad to help you with the puzzle. Or get someone to work on your awesome plans for the future. You know, those big, secret plans that you have to become a door-to-door geode salesman with your little brother; develop a wholesale candy business with your best friend at school; or build a magnificent fort with your cousins using nothing but the sticks and twigs in your backyard.

If geodes, candies, or forts aren't your thing, do whatever IS your thing. After all, it's the *people*, rather than the activities, that actually make you feel better. One way or another, find time to be with people who care about you. Whatever activity you choose—from the ordinary to the extraordinary—it's important to get a break from your phone screen and see the people you like and who like you. Bonus points if you can go outside.

Change who you follow and text with. If a certain social media app keeps bringing you down, you don't have to use it. Delete it from your phone! Or take a break from it for a while. Or change who you follow—delete those people who seem to gloat or hate all the time.

If texting with that kid from the skate park always seems to make you anxious, sad, or angry, don't text with that kid anymore. You can even block their number. If a group chat you're in is getting testy or gives you FOMO, drop out of that chat. Or ask your friends to change the way they use it. You can make healthy choices FOR YOU.

Ask a grown-up for help. Grown-ups might not have had smartphones when they were your age, but they still had hard times with friends. Try asking a grown-up you trust about times that they might have felt left out, excluded, or lonely. Sometimes just hearing how someone you admire got through a situation similar to yours can make you feel better. The grown-up might even have some advice for dealing with your situation.

If you feel really blue or lonely, or if you feel like hurting yourself, please talk to an adult you trust right away. It could be your parents, other relatives, your teacher, or even your doctor. You don't have to go through this alone.

Bonus
Download

➜ It's normal to feel worried sometimes. That happens to everyone. Most of the time your phone is fun, but sometimes it can add to your worries.

➜ Because phones are so quick, sometimes we worry when someone is slow in responding to our message. But the other person might be at practice, doing chores, or napping! Take a deep breath and give your friends a little time to respond.

➜ Instead of FOMO—Fear of Missing Out—see if you can see things in a different way. What about JOMO—Joy of Missing Out? Sometimes it can be nice to just relax and focus on a game with your family or gaze up at the clouds in the sky. Those moments can be joyful!

Chapter 6

Screaming Babies Aren't the Only Ones who Need to Sleep: Healthy Life Balance

Are you a tech zombie? It's starting to get late, but you're still really into the show that you're watching, and you want to watch just ONE MORE EPISODE.

Or, you're trying to post your latest lip-syncing vid, and you've *almost* got it edited perfectly. Maybe your mom has yelled upstairs a few times. Maybe you've gotten your "FIVE MORE MINUTES" warning. You're tired. You're sleepy. Your eyeballs are getting sore and itchy, but you're having fun online. Maybe you can just hide under the covers and finish this up . . .

And it isn't just about bedtime. You're feeling sucked in by that phone all day. It's like a giant vacuum cleaner that sucks up your time. You watch a video, and it's super cool, and when it's over another video auto-plays, and then another after that, and then another . . . and then another.

(And then another.)

That greedy vacuum cleaner doesn't care if you're gotten any exercise; it doesn't care if you've slept or eaten dinner; it doesn't care that you have homework; it doesn't care if you haven't been outside in the last 72 hours. In fact, some applications are actually *designed* to suck you in and not let you go. Imagine if other things in life were on auto-play like those videos. As soon as you finished one dessert, somebody put another dessert right into your mouth. You finish that one, here comes another—and so on. At first, it would be amazing. But after about six slices of cake, you might start to feel sick.

Planning for Life Balance

Actually, it's not just a few apps that are designed to keep you engaged in your phone. The phone itself is an addictive device. All those bright icons, flashing and beeping notifications, the endless scroll-ability of social media and messaging—the content never ends. The whole concept of phones is to keep you on your phone.

In fact, studies show that people often respond to their phones—those notifications and messages—with the same speed, urgency, and care that they would normally reserve for a screaming baby. How stressful!

It should be no surprise that lots of kids find it hard to manage their time after they get a phone. If it's hard to stay off your phone, then you end up spending a LOT of time on it. And as you know, there are only 24 hours in a day. If you spend too many of those hours watching videos, playing games, texting friends, checking social, watching more videos, posting selfies, playing games, and oh yeah watching MORE videos, then you aren't spending those hours doing important things like exercising, homework, socializing, or playing with pets.

You need to be able to manage your phone. This is called having a healthy life balance. A good way to start is by setting yourself some rules about when you'll turn your phone off. Here are a few ideas:

- Turn your phone over to a parent in the evening. That way you won't be tempted to look at it when you should be getting ready to sleep or actually sleeping.

- Keep your phone in a different room when doing homework. That way you won't get distracted by notifications telling you that there's something really, really important you have to pay attention to, like a picture of a cute otter.

- Make a family rule about no phones at the dinner table. This helps to make sure that when your family is together, you talk to each other. That's important.

- Leave your phone at home or at the bottom of your backpack when you walk the dog, go to school, and do other things outside your home. You know you don't really need it for math class or volleyball practice.

If your phone is sucking up too much of your life, ask an adult to help you set some guidelines.

Are You Feeling Sleepy?

One of the most important life balance challenges that kids and adults face is getting enough sleep. To help you understand, here comes a fancy, school-ish word. (Though, to be fair, some fancy words are definitely NOT something you would learn at school, like *flatulence*, which means farting, or *emetic,* which is something that makes you . . . um . . . blow chunks. Try those beauties on the adults in your life sometime. They'll be delighted—promise!)

But the fancy word for today is *biology,* which basically means the study of life. Here's a biology lesson: **All animals need to sleep.** That includes people. Sleep is how humans process stress, refresh their minds, rest their weary bodies, and get ready to do it all again the next day.

Did you know that *not* sleeping enough makes you crankier, less smart, not as much fun, and maybe even overweight? Not getting enough sleep can make you feel lousy. Not sleeping enough can make you feel tired, flopsy, and disinterested. It can make it hard for you to concentrate or pay attention—even to things that you love, like grilled cheese. It can even make you feel sad or depressed.

Important question. Do you know what part of the body figures out if it's time to go to sleep?

Did you guess your brain? That would be a good guess, but it would also be . . . WRONG!

Well, PARTLY WRONG! Your brain eventually gets the message. But the part of your body that *sends* the message is your eyes—specifically the backs of your eyeballs.

Yes, even though it sounds strange, the back of your eyeball tells your brain whether it's daytime or nighttime. Whether it's time to be awake or time to be asleep. And how do the backs of your eyeballs know what time it is?

By responding to light that comes into your eyes.

What does all this have to do with your new phone?

Hmm, does it give off a lot of light?

Yes. Yes it does. So, when you are looking at your bright-as-day screen, what do you think your eyeballs are reporting to your brain?

Hey, Brain! Why are you so sleepy? It's time to be awake! It's time for playing! Time for being alert! Stay awake, you!

Your frenetic, bellowing eyeballs, tricked by the extreme brightness of your screen, tell your brain that it's time to be awake. And it's not just any light that's coming from your screen, by the way. It's blue light. You see, visible light comes in a spectrum of colors: red, orange, yellow, green, blue, indigo, and violet. Put them all together, and you get white light—the light you see coming from the sun.

Devices such as smartphones, tablets, and TVs put off a lot of blue light. There is evidence that blue light is good for things like helping us be alert, improving our memory, and even improving our mood. However, it is *not* good for other things. For one thing, too much blue light may raise your risk of eye disease. For another, blue light makes it hard to sleep.

REALLY hard to sleep. . .

And as you know, since you are an *animal,* you need sleep. Experts say that kids your age need 8 to 10 hours a day. If you don't get enough sleep, you wake up looking like this . . .

So what can you do about this? Are you supposed to never look at your phone screen again? That's a really brilliant idea. Maybe while you're at it, you could never look at the TV again and never look at the toilet to aim when you're . . . never mind.

The Solution to Light Pollution

With all these jokes about bodily fluids, you may have missed the central point. Well, here it is: You can't use your phone or tablet or screen and then expect to go right to sleep. The light is too bright. After you turn the screen off, it takes an hour or two for your brain to really settle down for restful, rejuvenating sleep.

The solution is to get off your technology at least an hour before bedtime.

If you've gotten in the habit of taking your phone to bed at night, this might sound really hard to do. If your friends are texting and posting late into the evening, it can be extra hard. You might feel some of that FOMO you read about in the last chapter. The trick is to make a bedtime plan.

Plan to charge your phone in a different room at night. Some families have a station in their kitchen where everyone leaves their devices until morning. This is your best bet for getting good sleep.

Turn on the "Do Not Disturb" function on your phone. This is the second-best option. Maybe you're reading a book, and you swear you're not going to check your phone, but you like to use your phone to play some soft music. If you think you can handle the temptation, go ahead and use your phone to play music in your room. But make sure to turn on "Do Not Disturb." That way you won't get any notifications, so you won't be tempted to answer them.

Use "Nighttime Mode." Do you like to read on your device? Oh, boy, it really requires some discipline to only read and NOT switch over to texting or social media. Again, "Do Not Disturb" is your friend. You can also change the settings on your phone to "night mode." That lowers the amount of blue light your phone puts off. In fact, on most phones you can set it to automatically turn to nighttime mode every night.

You might also want to try blue light glasses. No, they do not shoot blue light out of the lenses like a sci-fi villain. They are snazzy glasses that *block* blue light. That way your brain still gets the message that it's nighttime—time to sleep.

Of course, in the end, there's one trick that always works: It is never a bad idea to just take a break from your phone. Like, actually TURN IT OFF. Give your brain, your eyeballs, and your scrolling finger a break, especially at night. Don't worry, all those messages and posts and videos will still be there when you turn it on again.

Bonus
Download

➤ *Life balance* means that no matter how much fun your new phone is, you still need to rest, sleep, eat, do your homework, go outside, and play with your dog.

➤ Your phone is a great tool for having fun *and* doing constructive things like reading about volcanoes or learning to speak Spanish. But no matter what you're doing, beware that cell phones can "vacuum up" all your free time if you're not careful.

➤ But let's not give vacuums a bad rap. They weren't created to suck up time. Did you know that vacuums are used to make light bulbs, do scientific experiments, and even to cut hair? And they were first invented as a way to *dry* hair. Imagine someone using the family vacuum to style their hair every morning. That would be quite a sight!

Chapter 7

Kids Can Do AWESOME Things with Their Phones: And So Can You!

You've heard all about how having a phone is a BIG responsibility. Your parent might remind you of this all the time. But having a smartphone is more than a BIG responsibility, and it's more than a daily *lack-of-pep* talk. You know it's actually really useful, exciting, and fun. An even cooler thing about your phone? Your family gave it to you because you have proved that you are responsible. They trust you. That's awesome, and it means you're growing up into a pretty awesome kid.

With your smartphone, you can learn about things you never imagined before. You can make new friends and bring old friendships to a whole new level. You can find new ways to be creative and goofy. Or creative and serious!

A Few Awesome Kids

Did you know that Marley Dias began a Twitter hashtag called *#1000BlackGirlBooks* to bring more attention to books featuring Black girls? And Greta Thunberg used the internet to organize her Fridays for the Future, where kids protest around the world for stronger action on climate change. Nicholas Lowinger created the website *Gotta Have Sole*, which makes sure that all kids get shoes. And Bana al-Abed has been using Twitter to let others know what it's like to be a kid today in Syria.

All these kids found important and inspiring uses for their phones, and you can too.

Jane: My youth group organized online, and now we read books to little kids.

Jamal: That's really awesome—like awesomely awesome.

Jane: Eloquent as ever.

Jamal: Did you hear about how Farhad used his phone to create a website and sell soap to raise money for the food bank?

Jane: I did. My family bought some. I also saw how Grace and Ellie organized a cleanup of the creek, shot videos with their phones, and posted them online to raise awareness.

Jamal: So much awesome.

Helping Others Is Awesome

You don't need a phone to do awesome things. You know that. But phones can make things easier. And they can help you elevate your awesomeness to new levels.

One way to be awesome with your phone is to help others.

First, think about WHOM you'd like to help. Are you interested in helping puppy dogs or iguanas? How about other kids? Maybe you'd like to help reduce bullying, or you want to help your school get the money for a field trip. Do you like reading? Do you like math? Maybe you can help other kids with their math homework. Use your phone to research different causes, and think about what you really like and what really interests you.

Second, think about HOW you'd like to help them. Does your religious community need help designing a website? Does a neighborhood news site need someone to take pictures at soccer games? Does your piano teacher need someone to record their practicing to share with others online? All these are easy, safe, and appropriate ways that you can use your phone to be helpful.

Being Creative Is Awesome

If creating is more your thing, you can use your phone to create content just for yourself or to share with others. Maybe photography sounds exciting to you. If so, your phone probably has a great camera on it, and you can find inexpensive or free photo editing apps in an app store. You can find how-to videos on YouTube. Give it a shot!

Other ways to be creative with your phone include:

- Shoot a dance video with your friends.

- Make up a scavenger hunt where everyone has to take a photo of items on the list, like a fir tree, a piece of art, a duck, three friends making a human pyramid, and so on.

- Record a podcast where you talk about something you love or that's important to you. You can publish it—or not! It's up to you.

- Make a drawing on a maps app by recording your walk in the neighborhood. See if you can walk in the shape of a kitten or a poop emoji.

- Make a song with a music app, or record yourself playing a song on guitar.

- Start a photo blog about a topic you care about.

You can probably come up with a million other ideas. Think about what interests you, what you'd like to create, and how your phone can help you get it done.

Ask That Trusted Adult

You know the grown-up you've talked to about some important things as you read this book? You can ask that person for some ideas about being awesome. Maybe they can tell you about something interesting or fun or helpful that they did when they were young. Maybe they'll have some ideas for how a phone might make doing that even better.

Or maybe they've heard stories about other kids doing exciting things with their phones. If they do, those ideas might inspire you to try something similar. Hey, maybe they'd like to do something awesome *with you*.

Someday, a kid might ask their mom or dad about another awesome kid they've heard of, and maybe that awesome kid will be YOU.

Bonus
Download

→ Kids can be really important in changing the world! You can use your phone to do awesome things. This chapter has lots of suggestions, but you'll likely invent some ideas all on your own. The point is your phone is an amazing tool for being creative and spreading positive messages. You are an awesome kid and an awesome smartphone user!

→ Your phone can help you with many of your hobbies! A digital library app means you can take dozens of books everywhere with you. Mapping apps can guide your walks, hikes, and other travel. You can find apps for storytelling, fitness, nature trails, gardening, stargazing, drawing, photography, podcasting, making music, making videos, learning geography, following sports . . . you get the idea!

→ Don't forget that your phone is also a way that you can keep safe and let your parents know where you are. So if your mom wants you to check in, check in. If your dad calls you, answer your phone.

Resources

Eric Braun, *Surviving Social Media: Shut Down the Haters.* Compass Point Books, 2020.

Blake Hoena, *Cell Phones and Smartphones: A Graphic History.* Graphic Universe, 2021.

Phyllis Kaufman Goodstein and Elizabeth Verdick. *Stand Up to Bullying! (Upstanders to the Rescue!).* Free Spirit Publishing, 2014.

KidsHealth: Online Safety
kidshealth.org/en/kids/online-id.html

Ray Reyes, *Smartphone Movies (Make It!).* Rourke Educational Media, 2018.

Trevor Romain and Elizabeth Verdick, *Cliques, Phonies, and Other Baloney.* Free Spirit Publishing, 2018.

Trevor Romain and Elizabeth Verdick, *Stress Can Really Get on Your Nerves.* Free Spirit Publishing, 2018.

Safe Search Kids: A Teen's Guide to Social Media Safety
safesearchkids.com/a-teens
-guide-to-social-media-safety

Index

About the Authors and Illustrator

Elizabeth Englander is a college professor who has spent more than 25 years doing research and thinking about ways to help kids be happier, less worried, and make more friends as they grow up. She's written eight books and about a hundred really nerdy, technical articles in research journals. She likes writing, riding her bike, and very noisy power tools. She has an equally nerdy husband and three kids and lives in Boston, Massachusetts.

Katharine Covino is a college professor who teaches teachers how to teach. She's been a teacher for almost 20 years. She's interested in finding ways of helping young teachers who are just starting out. She also writes about her work asking young kids interesting and tough questions. She believes that all students should be able to see themselves reflected in the books and stories they read. When she's not teaching or writing, Katharine tries to keep up with her kids. Despite her very best efforts, they are all faster swimmers, hikers, and skiers than she is. She also tries to make them laugh, and sometimes she is successful. Katharine lives near Boston, Massachusetts.

Steve Mark is a freelance illustrator and a part-time puppeteer. He lives in Minnesota and is the father of three and the husband of one. Steve has illustrated many books for children, including all the books in the Laugh & Learn® series and the Little Laugh & Learn™ series for younger kids.

Free Spirit's
Laugh & Learn® Series

Solid information, a kid-centric point of view, and a sense of humor combine to make each book in our Laugh & Learn series an invaluable tool for getting through life's rough spots. For ages 8–13. *Paperback; 80–136 pp.; illust.; 5⅛" x 7"*